A

The poems in this book fo
page they reside on is the
Read page by page, or flip
the book, you will find pages that have been intentionally left
blank. This is a space for your own words to come alive. On
every other page, you will find a prompt. This is to inspire
your creativity, however, do not let this limit you and ignore
them completely if you desire.

At the age of 18, I was diagnosed with borderline personality
disorder, something that is difficult for many to understand. I
always had trouble articulating my emotions because of their
intense nature, but writing has been an effective way for me
to speak on the difficulties I experience in relationships,
family, friend dynamics, and mental health.

Since the age of 12, I have tackled my way through
inpatient/outpatient mental health services. It took a great
amount of time for me to find answers on why I did not think
and act like everyone else. Nobody understood me, nobody
could help me, nobody had the patience for me. Now, at the
age of 21 when this book was written, things are much
clearer. Although I struggle most days, I know that I can
make a life for myself that is worth living, and I know you
can too.

This collection of modern poetry is for those just like me, and
even those who are not. Take what resonates, leave the rest,
and *always* take care of yourself.

Yours truly,
Keira

Diary of a Borderline

Copyright © 2023 KEIRA Van der Kolk
All rights reserved

Borderline
that is what they call it
Constantly dancing on the thin line of feeling absolutely everything
and then nothing all at once
Borderline
the evil occupying my mind
I do not recognize myself half of the time
and even if I could
I do not think I would want to
Borderline
this body feels like a prison
my bones are metal bars
my flesh resembles everything I do not want to be
Borderline
but all I hear is misunderstood
unwanted
unseen
Borderline
and how am I supposed to leave
It has made a home inside of me

Diary of a Borderline

How come
I do not know what love feels like
but I know heartache
so well?

Keira Van der Kolk

Eventually I got tired of waiting for you
even though it still pains me to know
that I will never be that person for you
The one you tell all your troubles to
the one you share all your happiness with
I accept it now
but every once in a while
I break
just a little bit more

It is exhausting really
Falling apart each time I feel our love changing
even if it is not
It always feels like the end of the world
at least twice a day
so I apologize
for being a different type of lover than you are used to
but I will never apologize
for how hard
I will love you

You set a fire
to my heart
lit the match and watched me burn
from the inside out
A merciless arsonist
I saw the look on your face
as you watched me plead
You wanted it this way
you never intended to hold my heart
with care
I should have known
that the moment I gave you all of me
I would soon be turned
to ash

Diary of a Borderline

It killed me when we fought
But now that you are gone
I would give absolutely anything
to fight with you once more
And if I had the chance
I would go through all this heartbreak again
just so I could hold you one last time
because despite the way we ended
I am utterly blinded
by the way I felt
when we started

Keira Van der Kolk

It was never love
not even for a moment
All I did was fuel you
all you did was feed off me
until I was empty
until there was nothing left of me

Diary of a Borderline

If you were to ask him
if he broke my heart
I do not even think he would consider me someone to break
Crumbling in his palms
and calling it fate
calling it everything I have ever wanted
Maybe I am a liability
for thinking he loved me enough
to not love me anymore

Keira Van der Kolk

I wondered what it would be like
to be kissed without expectation
without wandering hands down my shirt
without temptation
or aggression
I wondered
what it would feel like
to be loved
just for the sake of being loved
not when I was undressed
on my knees
or in any other form
that is not what I already am
with the lights turned on

Diary of a Borderline

He told me do not be vanilla
so I let him put his hands on me
but not in a nice way though
because I thought it would make him like me
But I am convinced I only ever wanted it rough
because he conditioned me to believe that the time I look
most beautiful
is with his hand wrapped around my neck
he told me watching me look up at him
with lifeless eyes gets him off
so I compromised soft touch
and gentle hands
for hands that would rather grab me
and pull me
and expect me to be in two places
at once
And God forbid I want the type of kiss
that does not leave an aching
I told him tonight I do not want marks scattered on my skin
I want him to linger my heart with fingerprints
and he told me do not be vanilla
You see
I am afraid that the time I look most beautiful to him
is with my head
buried in the pillow

Being loved by you
was only ever something I longed for
because I had to fight so hard
to get it
to truly feel it
I thought I could never survive
without it
the only validation I needed to keep this heart beating
But real love does not need to be begged for
and you never really made me feel that special anyway

Diary of a Borderline

I cannot help but feel responsible
for my own heartache
I should have left
the first time around
instead of believing you changed
just because you said you did
Every time I caved back into your arms
I was willingly giving you more of me
in hopes that we would stick
But little did I know
all I did was help you
ruin me

Keira Van der Kolk

I do not know how to let go of people
without letting it
destroy me

Diary of a Borderline

I am tired of saying that you were my right person
wrong time
I know now that the only reason
those words escape my lips
is because I have been trying to heal these wounds
But pretending like we work out
in another lifetime
hurts more than accepting
that you and I
just were not right
at all

The difference between you and I
is that I saved myself
I picked up the pieces
I found a way to live again
But you were too busy
drowning your sorrows in God knows what
trying to repair what you broke
the only way you know how
and I cannot get angry at you for that
But I hope you know
the person who hurts
does not get another chance at love
a real chance anyway
and the one that is left broken
will find love in everything
and will be loved back
every single time

I had to convince you
that I was good enough
to be cared for
As if gentle hands
were earned
not expected
kindness a privilege
never unprompted
intimacy one-sided
rarely exchanged
But that is not how love works
there is no persuasion
or begging to be kept
It is simple
and anyone who makes it complicated
does not love you

Keira Van der Kolk

If I do not have you in my hands
my body has no recollection of what it is like
to hold you
to be held by you
to be wanted by you
I am sorry for needing you so badly
the moment you leave
it is like you were never here
in the first place

Diary of a Borderline

I hate that he calls me pretty
and I forget everything he has ever done to me
like two syllables is simply enough
to take it all back
and in the moment it is everything
When he caresses my hair
traces my skin
and looks at me with purpose
So I will forget what he said to me
the night before
because right now
he is everything that I want him to be

Keira Van der Kolk

I hope I do not have a daughter
that is what he said to me
as he watched the young girl walking down the street
in a top just above her belly button
He looked at her in disgust
or was it lust
I do not know
lately the two coexist
Tell me why you hate my body
but want to take it from me
Why do you despise the size of my thighs
but every night you fantasize
Tell me about your obsession with the female form
your desire to clutch it in your palms
but once you do I am a whore
Tell me why you hate me so much
And he said
I just hope I do not have a daughter
to which I replied
God
I hope you do not either

Diary of a Borderline

There is a thin line
between the loneliness being comforting
and it being gutting
And I cannot decipher whether it is saving me
or killing me
I think it is both

After it ends
we are alike eventually
Stripped of this skin
comprised of the same substance
whether you were a bad person
or not
we both end up bone
And I do not know how to survive
knowing that despite all this pain
our destinies
will inevitably
be the same

Diary of a Borderline

I knew I loved you
when I begged the universe
not to take you from me
And I knew I loved you far too much
when I completely fell apart when she did

I do not think he liked me very much
actually
I think he liked me somewhat at some point
I am just not so sure when he stopped
actually
I felt him slipping away as he stood in front of me
even with his arms wrapped around me
it felt like his hands had some place they would just rather be
And I cannot seem to accept it
I hoped that he would realize eventually
that I am worth
being loved
but he never did

As every session begins
I dread the question that follows its end
do you feel safe?
I feel like blurting out the *no*
it burns a fire in my throat
I want to scream it at the top of my lungs
spew out every single way I thought of ending it
before it was even Tuesday
I tell her I am fine each time
because truthfully
what can she do if I am not
Another pill
another doctor
another *something*
to try and fix what we both know
needs far more than anything
she could ever give me
Maybe healing does truly begin
when you confront the thing
that is breaking you
but what can I do
if I am the very thing
that is breaking me?

Keira Van der Kolk

You are the reason
I clutch onto those I love
just a little too tight now

Diary of a Borderline

You called me the most beautiful thing
you have ever seen
and in the same breath
told me you did not love me anymore
Now I cannot help but question
when they compliment my eyes
or think they are changing their mind
when they look at me a little too long
Perhaps they really do think I am beautiful
that my eyes really do remind them of everything
they have ever loved
And when they look at me a little too long
it is simply because they cannot fathom ever looking
at someone else the same
You might have convinced me for a while that love was a lie
but they are living proof
that you could have not been any more wrong

Unfair
how easily you move
throughout the world without a care
And in case you were wondering
I am far too busy rotting away
between these four walls to even realize
there is even anything outside of them
Too busy sinking into these bedsheets
with a pounding chest
inhaling fear with each breath
You get to forget
how was it so easy for you to forget?
because each day I wake
all I can do is remember what you took from me

Diary of a Borderline

No one loves quite like a borderline
so I cannot hold it against you
for not loving me
the way I need you to
But I cannot help but hold it against myself
for expecting you to understand me
when I cannot even figure myself out
Why I do the things I do
why I cannot contain the things I feel
But maybe it is a good thing
the way I move through the world so loudly
quiet has just never been my thing
So it is true
no one loves quite like a borderline
but they can try

Keira Van der Kolk

This seems to be
how it always ends
how it will only ever end
You are fine
and my world is collapsing
over and over again

I could have turned cold-hearted
after it all
but I could not bear the thought
of becoming like you

Keira Van der Kolk

I think I have spent more time
thinking about death
far more than I have ever thought about living
graduating school
falling in love
and doing it right
Meeting the group of friends I spend forever with
the type that never make you feel out of place
not even for a moment
Moving away from my hometown
sinking my teeth into unfamiliarity
After awhile
thinking about death
gets tiring
and I do not want to spend each breath
waiting for the end
So when do I get to think about living?

People like you do not belong
with people like me
It is not that I am not worth it
it is that you are not
I tried so hard to make us work
to make you into someone
you will never be
I am ashamed
I wasted so much time
trying to see the good in you
And I do not mean to be conceited
but the only thing that was ever good about you
was me

Keira Van der Kolk

I am a lover girl
I like kisses on the forehead
and having my hand held in public
I like bundles of tulips or a singular rose
from your neighbour's garden
I like skin on skin contact and raw vulnerability
I am a lover girl
Enchanted by the bare minimum
and unsurprised when I receive less
I make excuses for slow texts
I stay awake all night because he says he'll call
I apply makeup just in case his plans change
I assure my friends he's not as bad as he seems
I am a lover girl
meaning I fall in love with people
who have no business being loved by me

Diary of a Borderline

When you left
I found peace
The loss of you
rarely feels like a loss to me

Keira Van der Kolk

You asks if we can still be friends
as my heart is still fresh in your hands
I wonder what else you will take from me
or what else I will be willing to give you
or how even with this void in my chest
all I can think is that if you do not love me
like you say
why do you care enough
to hurt me?

I am afraid I will die before someone tells me
that they love me
Pardon the pessimism
I know some might say there is more to life than that
and I am sure that is true
but it is a beautiful thing
being loved
Knowing that out of all the people in the world
all the possibilities
all the faces
and laughs
they chose to love you
to kiss you
to listen to you
I am sure there is something else out there
that someone finds just as beautiful
but to me
nothing is more beautiful than that

Keira Van der Kolk

It is hard for me to love you
Not in the way that beautiful people feel unlovable
but in the way that it drains me to my core
Not because you have the inability to see all that you are
or have stupid little habits like biting your nails
or somehow cry during a movie that is not even sad
It is because you do not know what it takes to love
It is because you only keep me around
to pry all the warmth out of me
suck the energy from my bones and make it your own
I can tell that all you see when you look at me
is temporary
and unconditional vulnerability
but I refuse to settle in your wrath anymore
and expecting comfort
or hoping the good day will last just another day
It is hard for me to love you
but not for the things that make you human
but for the things that make you unrecognizable

Diary of a Borderline

You have time
I know it does not seem like that right now
and I know you feel the need to make everyday count
but I promise you have time
The day can wait
Retire the productivity for a moment
let your body sink into the bedsheets
you did not spend all that money on them for nothing
Leave the blinds closed
the sunshine will not hold it against you
Put the anxiety in a box on the shelf
You have time
That text can wait
your friends will understand
eat 99-cent noodles
leave your hair in that bun
the shower will be there in the morning
I understand why you want to make everyday count
But if breathing is all that you are capable of today
I promise that counts for something

Keira Van der Kolk

I hope my mother knows how hard I tried
to be something more
than just skin and bones

Diary of a Borderline

I could tell you they felt like home
but I have been the unreliable narrator in this story
once before
I have looked into the eyes of red
and only managed to feel their warmth
I guess I could say they felt like home
because home to me is war
and they never held me softly enough
to convince me that love is anything more

Loving me is simple
I no longer believe
that I am hard to love
because truthfully
I am not at all
But they always made it seem like a chore
a task you dread to finish
I do not understand
because I never ask for much
or really anything at all
just soft touch
and they could not even give me that

Diary of a Borderline

I am not the same person
you cheated on
I do not submit to lovers
that cannot remember my favourite colour
I stopped collapsing into arms
that will not hold only me
I refuse to swallow my hurt
I no longer bury my needs beneath my feet
I am not the same person
I wanted you to appreciate
and I no longer desire to be

I am responsible for my own heartache
At one point you were to blame
but I keep pretending that I can somehow love you
into giving me a happier ending
So I give you more of me
stretch myself thin while you remain the same
I am to blame
but I would rather be the person who always loves
far too much
than ever be the person
who was afraid to even love
at all

Diary of a Borderline

I cannot remember when it stopped
that butterfly feeling in my stomach
All I know is that I was six once before
and then suddenly I was not
Growing up is not at all what I expected it to be
The first love
the first kiss
the first everything
apparently you do not get to skip the tear-stained cheeks
and anger-filled heart
My father called it a rite of passage
as if I were graduating from the eighth grade
but I wonder
why after all this time
I still break the same

Keira Van der Kolk

They teach you how to fall in love
but they never teach you
how to stop
So here I am
learning how to unlove you
And every day I forget you
a little bit more
but I think a part of me
will always love you
no matter how much time has passed

I do not know who you are anymore
and it hurts
but you do not know who I am anymore
either
and that is liberating

You never think you are capable of leaving
until you do
And you finally feel like yourself again
you find the pieces of you that you had lost
and everything starts to hurt less
You stop looking at the world with so much anger
that pit in your stomach dissipates
and you stop hating people that found their love so easily
when you have not
The one thing about leaving
is that it is painful at first
but nothing hurts more than sticking around
just in case they decide to love you the same

Diary of a Borderline

You have overstayed your welcome
and I think it is time you leave
I have never been good at letting go
but then again
you have never been good at loving me

They say a girl's father is always her first love
I know now why it has never come easy to me
I wondered if I had to fight so hard for him
who am I to try again?
They say a father teaches his daughter
how to be treated
I know now why I clutch onto any warmth
they are willing to give me
or why I so easily
find comfort in the chaos
I am not quite sure if my father is my first love
and I hope he is not
But one thing I know for sure
is that he is most definitely my first heartbreak

Diary of a Borderline

You are never going to love me
but there is still time
for me to love me

He is familiar with every inch of my skin
but my favourite colour always seemed to be
too intimate for him
And I think if I were to ask him
when my birthday is
he would probably stutter and drown in hesitation
Somehow I know him
from the inside out
but he never even bothered to acknowledge
that I was a human being too
and that a kiss on the forehead
meant something more to me

Even though we experienced
the same heartbreak
I seem to be the only one left bleeding
Perhaps we did not experience the same heartbreak
I just thought I meant more to you
than I actually did

Keira Van der Kolk

How many times did you touch me
and hold me close
all while knowing you did not want me anymore?
I often find myself wondering
which kiss was the last kiss you gave to me with love
and at what point they came from obligation instead
Ever since you left
I have trouble trusting new arms that want to hold me
because how will I ever distinguish
passion from guilt
when you blurred the lines so easily?

Diary of a Borderline

I still think about you
just a little bit differently now
I do not cling to the possibilities of us
and mourn the person you used to be
I do not wither in our memories
and hope you will come back to me
I just remember you kindly
and every once in a while
when I see something that reminds me of you
it does not make me sad
it makes me grateful to have known you

Keira Van der Kolk

He called me love today
and I thought of you
I have moved on
but I remembered the softness of your voice
when you called me that for the very first time
it is the sweetest thing I have ever known
and it sounded foreign coming from his lips
Even if I have moved on
I cannot help but settle in the memory of you
and I hate you for it

The Summertime comes around
and I feel alive once again
The greenery on the trees
reminds me of everything I want to be
vibrant and free
And if you want to find me
I will be happily getting lost
in the rays of the sun
falling in love with who I am
and not regretting who I was
It is finally the time
where I no longer just exist
but I live
vibrant and free

Keira Van der Kolk

We do not talk anymore
but we will never be strangers
we are just two people who once meant the world
to each other
and no amount of time
will ever make you unknown
because to have a love like we did
there is no forgetting that
and I mean truly forgetting it
Even if we never speak again
you will always be someone to me

Diary of a Borderline

I never knew going into this
that I would eventually have to heal from you

Keira Van der Kolk

It is true the world keeps spinning
and everyone keeps living
whether I am here
or not
But my favourite tea will sit lonely in the cupboard
because nobody else likes the taste of it
the new shoes I bought last weekend will remain unworn
And what about all of those books I own
that I have not read yet?
or the people I have not met?
Even if the world keep spinning
and everyone keeps living
there is still far too much for me to love right now
and far too much for me to savour

If I were to look back on who I was
this time last year
I do not think I could have predicted
finding someone like you
Someone so gentle
and loving
who takes care of me
and not because they want something in return
but because they want to
Someone who cannot handle watching me cry
and most definitely does not make me lay awake at night
wishing I were different
It truly is a beautiful thing
being loved right
after being loved wrong
for so long

Keira Van der Kolk

You knew all of me
and decided to love me
anyway
Saw the parts of me I would not dare to share
and chose me anyway
and that is the greatest love story
I have ever known

Diary of a Borderline

When you said forever
my heart knew you did not mean forever
but I still thought we had at least
a little more time together

Keira Van der Kolk

You think I cannot live without you
don't you?
You truly believe everything that I do
everything that I am
is all because of you
That I cannot sleep unless you are next to me
or I carry around this heavy feeling in my chest
until you call me back
or every time I try and move on it fails
because why would I want anyone else?
But you could not be any more wrong this time
I sleep just fine
I breathe just fine
and I think I am starting to fall for someone new
and I hope you do not take credit for the person I am
I did that all on my own

Diary of a Borderline

Kiss me in public
Hold me close even when no one is watching
and every once in a while try and pull me closer
as if there is something deeper than skin on skin
Let me talk about things that you do not necessarily care for
but let me go on for hours about them anyway
and learn to understand them the way I do
Do not be alarmed when I sob at videos of dogs being rescued
I am emotional but look at it as a good thing
it is always a good thing
Tickle my back until I fall asleep
Stand in the candle aisle of every store we walk into
and smell each one
Do the things you say you are going to do
And get to know ugly parts of me and love me anyway
because I promise
that I will love you

Keira Van der Kolk

Nothing in particular makes me sad
I just know that there must be more to my life than this
and I know that I will probably spend its entirety
searching for it
So do not ask why I am sad
the only thing I know
is that I am not happy

I believe we live many lives
on various timelines
but our soulmates stay the same and exist in different forms
each time
I think you are mine
because I swear I have met you in a past life
Your presence reminds me of home
it gives me reason to exist
and whenever you are out of reach I am homesick
You are the greatest love I have ever known
and I hope it is true that our soulmates stay the same
but if they do not
I will spend forever searching for you
in everyone

Keira Van der Kolk

My whole life I have been focused on surviving
so much so that I do not know who I am
I have shrunk myself down
to nothing but a name

Diary of a Borderline

I wish someone would love me right for once
so I do not have to be strong
I hate waiting for your call
I hate dissecting the words you say
and thinking everything you do
you do in spite of me
I want to feel beautiful
I want to feel adored
I want to feel safe
I do not want to wonder
when you are going to leave next
and spend every waking second
hoping you will come back
All I want
is for someone to love me properly
the first time around
but I am afraid that even if I am loved right
I will never believe it

Keira Van der Kolk

When I say that I will love you forever
I mean that I will love you until you tell me not to
Even then I probably would not stop
I would just do it in silence
but for now I will do it loudly and without hesitation
And some days you might think all I do is love you
and that is probably true
I do love a little too hard and a little too much
but I do not feel shameful admitting it
One thing I have learned about being heartbroken
is that I would never in my life
want someone else to feel that way
and because of that
I know that being loved by me is a beautiful thing

Diary of a Borderline

When I love it consumes me
so do not ever think you will leave me empty
even if you leave me
The love I give lingers
I put it into everything
so do not ever think you took anything
from me
The most beautiful thing about me
is that I do not need a reason to love
and no reason is good enough for me to stop
so do not ever think
the love I give
will not survive
long after you have gone

Keira Van der Kolk

I felt happy and sad
all at once
while in your arms
because I know it ends soon
it always does

I will continue to live this life
even if it is easier not to
I will continue to wake up with this pit in my stomach
because at least that means I care enough
to care more
I am grateful for that ache
because I remember once before I felt literally nothing at all
and that scared me
I have learned to appreciate feeling everything all at once
because that means I have not completely lost myself yet

Keira Van der Kolk

You did not love me
you just loved the way that I loved you
without labels
the questions
or expectations
and I mean I do it well
I have gotten pretty good at not getting anything in return
but I thought this time was different
I thought that maybe if I tried a little bit harder
I could convince you that I am something to lose
but not loving you hard enough was never my problem
it was letting you make me feel
like I was not something to lose

Diary of a Borderline

You are losing me
I know I have said it before but
I mean it this time
And when I look at you
I love you a little less
when you touch me I no longer get that feeling
in my stomach
and when you kiss me
I hate when you kiss me
I know I have said it before
but I have finally loved you
for far too long

There is more to life
than the person that could not love you right
or even love you at all
I mean it sucks
thinking someone is your everything and they do not even think of you
at night
in the morning
when they are busy
when they are bored
I get it
in the moment it feels like your world is ending and you wonder why they just will not love you back
but it is not about you
or even about them
they just are not yours
and you are not theirs
And when you think about it
I mean truly think about it
is it really such a bad thing?
Why would you ever want someone
who does not want you
the same way you want them?

Diary of a Borderline

You are no longer here
but at least that means I get to fall in love again
Start over with someone new
someone who deserves to be loved by me
I stopped mourning you when I realized
that if you were meant for me
you would have not left me this broken
you would have held me with gentle hands
apologize for making me cry
or not make me cry at all
The good thing about letting you go
is that I get another chance
to be loved right

Keira Van der Kolk

I will cry in my sister's arms until my head hurts
and there is nothing else to do besides sleep
I will go out with my friends and kiss random people
I find attractive just to never speak to them again
I will tell my mother I miss you
and I will swear to her that you miss me too
I will get new tattoos
change my hair a few times
maybe dye it a dark blue
I will think of you
with everything I do
but I will never again
beg someone to love me
the way that I begged you

We never exchanged I love you's
but I loved you
and I like to think you loved me too
The way you held me
strangers do not hold strangers that way
and they definitely do not look at each other
the way you looked at me
so deeply
so passionately
Maybe you only held me that way
because I was right in front of you
and you did not want to hold me
you just wanted somebody to hold
Yet all I wanted was you

Keira Van der Kolk

Today I decided to forgive you
but I am doing it for me
because every day that I hate you
I hate myself
You do not deserve anything more
even my hatred is far too generous
So I will forgive you
silently
but believe me
you no longer have any power over me

My mother asks why I always fall in love
with the wrong type of people
I tell her I do not mean to mistake lust for love
but I just cannot help myself
They do not love me
but they hold me like they do
they kiss me like they do
and sometimes they even tell me that they do
It is not that I do not know it is not true
I do
it is just that love and hate somehow feel the same
when you are aching

Keira Van der Kolk

I love, love
even when it ends I am grateful I had it
in the first place
Whether it ends beautifully
or in disaster
at least I loved
And the most wonderful thing about having it once
is knowing that I will have it again

He told me he was not ready
so imagine my hurt
when I found out he had fallen in love with her
I question myself
I question everything
Perhaps her hair is softer
and her skin is smoother
her teeth whiter
her laugh prettier
her body desirable
he can clutch it in his palms without any trouble
Maybe she is quieter
gentle
delicate
easy to understand
she does not move throughout the world with chaos
and does not carry the weight of everything
she has ever loved on her shoulders
I am nothing like her
but then again
she is nothing like me
And him not loving me
does not mean a damn thing

Keira Van der Kolk

You made the right choice
walking away
and leaving them behind for good
this time
I know you are anxious
and in pain
and probably feel like it will never end
that you will mourn them for as long as you breathe
you will not
And right about now
something inside you is probably telling you
that you will never find someone like that again
perhaps you believe you will never love again
you will
You might even be thinking about going back
sending a text and telling your friends it is for closure
they do not
and even if they did
they have already taken too much from you

Diary of a Borderline

I used to envy the people
that do not love
the same way that I love
But I refuse to be quiet
and subtle
I will love loudly
or not at all
No one can give you a love
quite like mine
so tender
yet so rough at the same time
You might wonder how someone could feel
everything so deeply
but you will never want it
any other way

Keira Van der Kolk

I am not the girl that you pick
I am not the girl that you spend the rest of your life with
and I accept it
But I am the girl that makes you want to change
that makes you think of who you are
who you have been
and who you want to be
The girl you think of in 20 years' time
when you look at your daughter and pray no one hurts her
the same way you hurt me
Maybe I am just the girl before the relationship
the one who loves you when you are broken
and puts you back together for your real lover
The one you take out all your anger on
so she is not the one crying herself to sleep
You will not choose me
but I do not care about being chosen anymore
I am just tired of being the healer
The one you talk to for hours
but never ask a single thing
the one you kiss but only privately
the one you love
but
just do not love enough

Diary of a Borderline

You had me
you had all of me
until you did not
but if I am being honest
a part of me will always belong to you
but I cannot let you know that
Because it hurts
being unconditionally yours
and knowing that you know
I would do anything for you
But I just cannot hate you
I would probably love you forever
if it were up to me
so I will do it from afar
in silence
but do not ever think
you will feel my love again

Keira Van der Kolk

I do not like who I am
but there was a time when I hated myself more
than I do right now
so I guess I can be grateful for that
I no longer hate the parts of me that I cannot change
or thought I should change
my only concern now
is not resenting who I used to be

Diary of a Borderline

You never made me feel like a person
more like a chore or a task you dread to complete
a burden
a roadblock
something that is just standing in your way
You never treated me like a person
more like a placeholder
a shoulder to cry on
a body to clutch onto whenever you feel lonely
I am not a person when I am with you
I do not think I am not much of anything at all
so I do not know why I cannot let go of you
I just wanted to be something to you

Keira Van der Kolk

I will love you
but I will not love you to death
I will accept your flaws
but I will not tolerate your abuse
I will stick around
but not while you ruin me
I am not a pit stop
you cannot come and go as you please
you will not take advantage of my vulnerability
And if you want to love me
then love me kindly
love me softly
love me with every fibre of your being
but do not love me half
do not love me with doubt
do not love me with hesitation
I think I am finally over being loved wrong
I think I am finally over settling
I think I am finally done
accepting everything I do not deserve
just because I do not want to be alone

And if I ever have to choose between love
and hate
I hope I choose love
every single time
without hesitation
I hope I do not let the weight of the world
interfere with my kindness

Keira Van der Kolk

I have to learn how to mourn you
without wishing you will come back to me in the end
I know you will not
I have made peace with that
but some part of me
some lonely
fucked up part of me
is still foolishly hopeful
that you secretly miss the way my hand felt in yours
How it fit so perfectly without trouble
How it always felt like we were the only people in the world
I know you do not
so I will not wait for you
but that part of me
that fucked up part of me
would not say no to you if you did
come back

Sometimes I wish you stayed
so you could see the person I am underneath
all of this sadness and anger

Keira Van der Kolk

I am not broken
you may have hurt me
but you did not break me
I will admit
I was not myself for a while
but I rarely stay that way
no amount of pain is worth it to me to change
I am the same
even when I am not
I will never let anyone ruin me
especially not you

Diary of a Borderline

I am a forethought
I am in the back of your mind
or not in it at all
I am not the person you think of
when something makes you happy
or the person you run to
when something makes you sad
I am not on a pedestal
or a priority
I do not even think I am a person to you
but I still love you
I still long for you
and I think of you when something
makes me happy
and I definitely want to run to you
when something makes me sad
But you do not notice me
you see me
but do not notice me
you touch me
but you do not hold me
you kiss me
but you do not *kiss me*
and I settle for it
because it is you

Keira Van der Kolk

What if I only ever feel alive
when you want me?
what if everything only makes sense
when you hold me?
when I feel loved by you
I am on top of the world
I can breathe easily
but the thing about that
is you always rip it away from me eventually
and suddenly
I do not know who I am
I do not want to be who I am
You cannot make homes out of people
well you can
but should not
and I did anyway
I made you my everything
so now
when I do not feel loved by you
I am nothing

I tried not to fall for you
I mean I really did
but girls like me are not capable
of not falling
and I fell hard when you kissed me
when you placed your hand on my cheek and pulled me in
closely
and stopped
for just a moment
to tell me how beautiful you thought I was
Even if you kissing me like that only meant
one thing
even if you only told me what I wanted to hear
I thought I could make it something more
but it is never anything more than a kiss
than a touch
than a desire
but girls like me are meant
to fall
even if that always means falling for the wrong one
We just have so much love
with no where to put it

Keira Van der Kolk

It is not that I stopped caring for you
or even stopped loving you
I just got tired of being sad
tired of waiting for you
tired of being disappointed by you
I still care for you
and still love you
just not the way I used to

Diary of a Borderline

I have always had this deep loneliness to me
the type of lonely
where even in a crowded room
my soul still feels misplaced
Even when I am surrounded by the people I love
I feel I do not belong
because I always care more
love more
feel more
They do not understand me
and I am afraid if they do
I will end up even lonelier than before

Keira Van der Kolk

Write about: growth

Diary of a Borderline

Keira Van der Kolk

Write about: what it is like to be loved by you

Diary of a Borderline

Keira Van der Kolk

Write about: reasons to stay alive

Diary of a Borderline

Keira Van der Kolk

Write about: finally moving on

Diary of a Borderline

Keira Van der Kolk

Write about: mental illness

Printed in France by Amazon
Brétigny-sur-Orge, FR